RACE
AND COLLEGE
SPORTS

BY DUCHESS HARRIS, JD, PHD
WITH TOM STREISSGUTH

Essential Library

An Imprint of Abdo Publishing | abdobooks.com

ABDOBOOKS.COM

Published by Abdo Publishing, a division of ABDO, PO Box 398166, Minneapolis, Minnesota 55439. Copyright © 2019 by Abdo Consulting Group, Inc. International copyrights reserved in all countries. No part of this book may be reproduced in any form without written permission from the publisher. Essential Library™ is a trademark and logo of Abdo Publishing.

Printed in the United States of America, North Mankato, Minnesota
092018
012019

Cover Photo: Liu Zishan/Shutterstock Images
Interior Photos: Rich Clarkson/Sports Illustrated/Getty Images, 5; AP Images, 10, 12, 27, 33; Stock Montage/Archive Photos/Getty Images, 15; University of Southern California/Collegiate Images/Getty Images, 17; Iowa State University Library Special Collections and University Archives, 20; Darrell Hoemann/Champaign News-Gazette/AP Images, 25; Barry Staver/The Denver Post/Getty Images, 30; David Stluka/AP Images, 35; Dave Martin/AP Images, 39; Jack Harris/AP Images, 41; Bettmann/Getty Images, 44; Hal Brown/AP Images, 46; iStockphoto, 49; David J. Phillip/AP Images, 53, 66; Stephan Savoia/AP Images, 54; Ed Reinke/AP Images, 56; Susan Sterner/AP Images, 60–61; Robin Alam/Icon Sportswire/AP Images, 71; Cheriss May/NurPhoto/Sipa USA/AP Images, 75; Isaac Brekken/AP Images, 78; John G. Zimmerman /Sports Illustrated/Getty Images, 81; Jim Mone/AP Images, 84; Elise Amendola/AP Images, 87; Charles Knoblock/AP Images, 91; Duane Burleson/AP Images, 93; Zack Wajsgras/The Daily Progress/AP Images, 96; Rick Scuteri/AP Images, 98

Editor: Patrick Donnelly
Series Designer: Craig Hinton

LIBRARY OF CONGRESS CONTROL NUMBER: 2018947974

PUBLISHER'S CATALOGING-IN-PUBLICATION DATA

Names: Harris, Duchess, author. | Streissguth, Tom, author.
Title: Race and college sports / by Duchess Harris and Tom Streissguth.
Description: Minneapolis, Minnesota : Abdo Publishing, 2019 | Series: Race and sports |
    Includes online resources and index.
Identifiers: ISBN 9781532116728 (lib. bdg.) | ISBN 9781532159565 (ebook)
Subjects: LCSH: College sports--United States--History--Juvenile literature. | Racism
    in sports--Juvenile literature. | Sports--Juvenile literature. | Race relations--
    Juvenile literature.
Classification: DDC 796.089--dc23

CONTENTS

CHAPTER ONE

WHITE BALL, BLACK BALL

It was March 19, 1966, and the end of the college basketball season was at hand. The national championship game was taking place that night, but no major television network was interested in showing it live. The starting time—10:00 p.m. Eastern—made it too late to air in prime time. None of the national networks wanted to pay for the rights to show the game at a different time. Instead, a much smaller company, Sports Network Inc., would tape the game on 16 mm film. Over the next days, fans in a few cities around the nation would get to watch the game on local television stations.

For its annual spring tournament, the National Collegiate Athletic Association (NCAA) had sent invitations to 22 teams. At the end of the final game, the winning team would hoist the trophy given to the best college basketball squad in the land.

Texas Western College and the University of Kentucky took the court at Cole Field House, in College Park, Maryland, to play for the title. The teams were evenly matched, but Kentucky had more big-game experience, and its coach was a living legend. Adolph Rupp had been leading the Wildcats since 1930 and had won NCAA championships in 1948, 1951, and 1958.

A NARROW ESCAPE

Separating the races wasn't only a custom in sports. In Mississippi, it was the law that schools and public facilities had to keep the races separate. In the early 1960s, Mississippi State University conformed to the law by banning its teams from playing against any black players. In 1963, the school won a bid to enter the NCAA basketball tournament. State senator Billy Mitts, former student body president of Mississippi State, got a court injunction that banned the team from leaving campus for its first-round game against Loyola University, an integrated team from Chicago, Illinois. However, the injunction papers had to be handed directly to coach Babe McCarthy for the injunction to have the force of law.

McCarthy had no intention of missing or forfeiting the game. Before he could be served with the injunction, he drove over the state line to Tennessee. The next morning, the team boarded a plane at a private airfield in Starkville, Mississippi. The plane stopped in Nashville, Tennessee, to pick up McCarthy, then took off for East Lansing, Michigan, the site of the game.

Mississippi State lost its game against Loyola. But things turned out all right. When the team's return flight landed, fans cheered as the players stepped off the plane. To the players, and this home-state crowd, basketball was basketball, no matter the opposing players' race.

In the first half, Kentucky took the lead. But the Texas Western Miners were running with them. The Miners played a careful, precise game with set plays and strong defense. They also hit their shots. At the final buzzer, Texas Western had 72 points on the board to Kentucky's 65. Another NCAA basketball championship was in the books.

But the game meant more than just a small university in western Texas winning a trophy. For the first time, a team with five black players in the starting lineup had taken the floor for an NCAA championship game. College basketball, and college sports, would never be the same.

THE LEGENDARY ADOLPH RUPP

Adolph Rupp was smart and tough, and his players followed instructions. Over decades, he had made the Kentucky basketball program into a consistent winner. However, Rupp also had his problems, including raised expectations. The Wildcats were supposed to win consistently and get an NCAA tournament invitation every spring. In addition, college basketball was not protected from the changes happening in the world beyond campus. In the 1960s, African Americans were demanding to have their civil rights recognized. Part of that recognition

RECRUITING WES UNSELD

Rupp had no problem traveling out of state in search of players. He had recruited new Wildcats from Ohio, Illinois, and New York. But his recruitment efforts in the black community were half-hearted, at best. One example was his effort to recruit Wes Unseld, a talented black player from Louisville, Kentucky, just down the road from the Wildcats' home in Lexington.

Rupp sent two of his assistants to visit Unseld's home. But the player was out of state, playing in a tournament, so they couldn't talk to him. Rupp didn't bother to show up himself, and the Wildcats missed out on Unseld, who went to star at the University of Louisville from 1965 through 1968. He averaged 20.6 points and 18.9 rebounds a game during his career and was an All-American in his last two seasons at Louisville.

would be equal opportunity to attend—and participate in sports at—colleges and universities throughout the country. This caused a problem for Rupp. John W. Oswald, the president of the University of Kentucky, and Governor Ned Breathitt both wanted Rupp to recruit black athletes to play for Kentucky.

Rupp reluctantly agreed. He wanted the best players he could find, but he knew there would be problems. Black players had helped the University of Cincinnati win the national basketball title in 1961 and 1962. However, Cincinnati was in Ohio, a northern state. The Southeastern Conference (SEC), which included Kentucky and nine other schools in the South, had no black players at all. There seemed to be an unwritten rule in force. No coach in the SEC had yet crossed that line.

DON HASKINS

El Paso, Texas, is a border town in the remote, arid desert of the southwest. But basketball coach Don Haskins had no trouble recruiting players from all over the country to play for him at Texas Western. In the 1965–66 season, the Miners' roster included players from New York, Indiana, Missouri, Kansas, and Michigan. Some were from big cities, while others were raised in the country. Some were black, and some were white.

Don Haskins, center, *receives congratulations after his Texas Western Miners won the 1966 NCAA basketball title.*

What they had in common, Haskins knew, was ability. For that 1966 championship game, he started five black players against the all-white Kentucky squad. Haskins had no institutional pressure to worry about in the matter of race—Texas Western was an independent school that didn't belong to the SEC or any other athletic conference.

There was no reason for the coach to doubt himself, about this decision or any others. He was a winner. In his 38 years at Texas Western (which was later renamed the

University of Texas at El Paso), he would end up with only five losing seasons. His teams made 13 NCAA tournaments and finished with a record of 719 wins and 353 losses. "I wasn't out to be a pioneer when we played Kentucky," Haskins observed later in his career. "I was simply playing the best players on the team, and they happened to be black."[1]

He would hear about the 1966 team for years afterward. African Americans approached him in public to congratulate him for the win and express their gratitude for the starting team he put on the floor. He also received bushels of hate mail. Despite the advancement promoted by the civil rights movement, it seemed much of the country was not entirely ready to root for an all-black basketball team.

SOUR GRAPES

Rupp didn't take the loss to Texas Western in the NCAA 1966 championship very well. For years, he complained about the players Haskins started, expressing his opinion that several members of the Miners' lineup were, somehow, not fit to take the floor against his Wildcats.

In an interview nine years later, Rupp claimed his biggest disappointment was "not winning in '66 and finding out Texas Western had all those ineligible players . . . one was on parole from Tennessee State Prison. Two had been kicked out of a junior college in Iowa. Texas Western was suspended by the NCAA for three years after that."[2] Rupp's memory was faulty— Texas Western was never on probation or suspended by the NCAA, and the former prisoner of Rupp's imagination was actually a transfer student from Tennessee State University.

Kentucky basketball coach Adolph Rupp, left, was slow to adapt to desegregation in college basketball.

RULES AND RACE

The integration of college sports has played out over decades. Even after the question of integrated sports teams was settled, the issue of racism still burned in the NCAA rules governing college players. The organization holds to the concept of "student-athletes" who should earn nothing from their ability except a scholarship and spending money.

In the meantime, the market for certain college sports, especially basketball and football, is hot. These sports earn the schools, collectively, billions of dollars in revenue—much of it funneled through contracts for television rights negotiated by the NCAA and its member conferences and schools. Given that many of the student-athletes are racial minorities playing for well-paid (and mostly white) coaches and administrators, it's no surprise that race remains an issue in college sports.

Why do NCAA rules ban player agents? Why can't student-athletes accept gifts or financial help? Why don't they have the right to sell their image to advertisers or their autographs to fans? Why do players have to sit out for one year after switching schools? Why are NCAA athletes denied the right to earn the money they're really worth?

These are all the NCAA's rules, not public laws. In the opinion of some, they violate the basic constitutional and legal rights of the players. And they demonstrate that the historical disparity between the races in America has not ended but only changed its form. Racism, in this view, still thrives in college sports.

DISCUSSION STARTERS

- The NCAA bans agents for student-athletes. Would hiring an agent give an athlete an unfair advantage against other players who have no representative?
- What do you think were Adolph Rupp's reasons for not successfully recruiting black players at Kentucky?
- Why did white politicians object to college teams in their state competing against black athletes?

CHAPTER TWO

NOT PLAYING FAIR

When college sports teams began competing with each other in the late 1800s, students organized their sports teams. Football, baseball, rowing, and track and field were among the major sports. The Ivy League schools—prestigious East Coast colleges including Harvard, Yale, and Princeton—were the first to stage games and organize a league. Over the years, schools were able to generate a lot of money by selling game tickets to the public.

As the games began pulling in bigger crowds, newspapers began covering college sports. A large audience grew outside of the ivy-covered campus walls. Crowds filled the Yale Bowl and other big venues, and sports became much too profitable to leave to the students. College administrators and faculty decided adult supervision was needed.

At this time, there were few African Americans enrolled in northern universities and colleges. There were some historically black schools, in both the North and the South, that fielded their own teams. Largely, the races didn't mix on the field. Predominantly white southern colleges did not admit black students and would not allow their teams to compete against African Americans.

The University of Southern California had one of the few integrated college football teams in the late 1800s.

ORGANIZING SPORTS

College athletes, particularly football players, found mayhem on the field. Compared to today's game, there were fewer rules governing play and much less in the way of body protection. A few football players wore thin leather helmets, which didn't do much to protect their heads from violent blows and concussions. Every year, a few footballers lost their lives playing the game.

Eager for lurid stories that would sell their newspapers, sports editors covered the many fights, injuries, and deaths in detail. Strangely, the sensational stories only seemed to increase game attendance and popular interest. But they also inspired a call to action from President Theodore

Roosevelt. Something had to be done, Roosevelt insisted, about the oversight of college athletics in general. The president organized a meeting of college heads at the White House to talk over the situation. Nothing came of the meeting right away, but there would be major changes to college athletics in the years to come.

In the matter of organizing sports, Roosevelt's White House conference did not go far enough for Henry MacCracken, the chancellor of New York University (NYU). MacCracken invited all the heads of college football programs to a national conference to study the question of whether college athletics should be abolished.

The result was a Rules Committee, which then led to the forming of the Intercollegiate Athletic Association (IAA). When the IAA first organized, there were 62 members. In 1910, it became the National Collegiate Athletic Association, or NCAA.

THE DEADLY SPORT

Football was born from the English game of rugby, which had a well-deserved reputation as a dangerous sport. Rugby players took pride in their bruises and injuries, but in the early 1900s, football could also be fatal. Serious injuries and concussions were common in the era when padded leather helmets were the only means of protecting heads. Players came off the field with broken legs and arms, ruptured spleens, and torn knee ligaments. Others went to the hospital with broken collarbones or paralyzing spinal injuries. And a few met their ends. In 1905, 18 college football players died because of injuries suffered on the field.[1]

The purpose of the NCAA seemed straightforward enough: to make the rules. In later years, its role became much more prominent. The NCAA took control of the recruitment of high school athletes by colleges and the eligibility of these athletes to continue playing once they arrived on campus.

THE LEGEND OF JACK TRICE

The dangers of football did not deter Jack Trice. Nor did racism. Born and raised in a small Ohio town, Trice enrolled at Iowa State University, where he was recruited by coach Sam Willaman—his former high school coach—to join the football team. He was the only black player on the squad. It was 1923, and in those days, coaches played big, strong linemen such as Trice on both sides of the ball: offense as well as defense.

Trice hit hard and ran out every play. An enthusiastic local newspaperman reported: "Jack Trice, the big colored boy from Cleveland, looked like a mountain in the line being in every play, no matter whether it was a pass, plunge, end run or punt."[2] After a strong game against Simpson College at Iowa State's home field, Trice was named by Coach Willaman as a starter for the Cyclones' first road game, against the University of Minnesota. The Golden Gophers were one of the few college squads willing to compete against a team with black players.

Jack Trice, second from left, stands with his teammates in 1923.

By a set of laws and traditions known as Jim Crow, white and black people were separated in public places in certain areas of the country. Jim Crow rules extended to college sports, as well. Many college teams, especially those in the South, refused to play against teams with nonwhite players. For those who held to Jim Crow, there was a danger in putting the races on an equal footing on the football field, or anywhere else.

Although there was no governing body in place to enforce the unwritten rule, the colleges did have a "gentlemen's agreement." They segregated their teams, not wanting to miss or forfeit games over the issue. Among some Southern universities, a strict separation of the races in college sports continued until the 1970s.

Trice joined the Iowa State team for the train journey 200 miles (320 km) north to Minneapolis, Minnesota. A heavy responsibility weighed on his broad shoulders. He wasn't playing just for the Cyclones; as the first black varsity player at Iowa State and the only black player on the field in Minneapolis, he knew he would be representing an entire race. In his hotel room, on the eve of the game, he wrote:

> *The honor of my race, family and self are at stake. Everyone is expecting me to do big things. I will! My whole body and soul are to be thrown recklessly about the field tomorrow. Every time the ball is snapped, I will be trying to do more than my part.*[3]

In the third quarter, while playing defense against a Gophers pass play, Trice got into a tackling scrum. These massive pile-ons were a legacy of English rugby, from which the American sport of football was derived. The punching, kicking, and general mayhem that took place as players fought for control of the ball caused many of the sport's injuries and deaths.

On this play, Trice attempted a roll block, throwing his body horizontally across the ground. This was one of the most dangerous maneuvers in football. As often happened when a player was lying prone on the ground, several opposing players trampled Trice.

Unable to continue playing, Trice was taken to the university hospital for observation. He had suffered serious internal injuries, but he asked to return to Ames, Iowa, on the train with his teammates. A few hours later, the doctors released him. Back in Ames, Trice struggled with a bruised abdomen that grew infected. Two days later, he died.

GENTLEMEN'S AGREEMENT LIVES ON

The cause of Trice's death is still up for debate. Resentful of his presence on the field, the Minnesota players may have been trying to get Trice out of the game. The Ku Klux Klan, a secretive group founded in the South that opposed any mixing of the races, had growing support in the Midwest. Three schools had already refused to play against Iowa State in the 1923 season if Trice was allowed to play.[4]

Trice's death did not end the gentlemen's agreement. In 1939, Clemson, a South Carolina school, demanded that Boston College not play its black running back, Lou Montgomery, in the Cotton Bowl game. Boston College agreed. Harvard, Rutgers, and the University of Michigan also had agreed to requests to bench their black players.

However, as college sports became a big business, competition between schools brought about a change in attitudes. Colleges that recruited the best players regardless of their race turned out the best teams. Southern schools began to integrate, and their sports teams began fielding minority players.

With black players finally being allowed to play, new issues arose. They did not involve the separation of the races or equal opportunity for nonwhite players. The issues had to do with the NCAA, its many rules, and the big money earned by the schools, the leagues, the coaches—money that went everywhere, in fact, except to the players.

DISCUSSION STARTERS

o President Roosevelt's conference on college athletics resulted in the founding of the NCAA. Was this a positive or negative development?

o What factors do you think were most important in ending the gentlemen's agreement?

o Why do you think Jack Trice was so determined to play well against Minnesota?

CHIEF
ILLINIWEK

One of the first college mascots was Chief Illiniwek of the University of Illinois. He was created in the 1920s by Robert Zuppke, the school's football coach, when the university adopted the Fighting Illini as the nickname for its sports teams. Zuppke came up with the name Illiniwek and the mascot to represent the Peoria, a Native nation historically local to central Illinois.

The university chose student Webber Borchers to play Chief Illiniwek in the late 1920s. In need of a costume, Borchers traveled to the Pine Ridge reservation in South Dakota and hired a Dakota woman to put it together. The result was an ornate outfit complete with a buckskin shirt and an eagle-feather war bonnet. It matched a stereotype of Native American dress seen in cowboy movies and in popular western novels. But it had nothing to do with what the Peoria wore or had ever worn.

At Illini football games, Chief Illiniwek stormed the field on a charging horse. Letting out a fearsome scream, he flung a flaming spear to the middle of the field to mark the start of the game. This tradition lived on for decades.

Native Americans at the University of Illinois and elsewhere saw the costume and the pregame spectacle as an insult. They especially objected to traditional religious symbols—such as eagle feathers—being used to promote the sports teams.

But Chief Illiniwek soon had plenty of company. Other universities employed mascots depicting Native Americans

University of Illinois mascot Chief Illiniwek performs at a football game in 2005.

in stereotypical fashion, such as the Florida State Seminoles, Stanford Indians, and St. John's Redmen. Professional teams adopted Indian mascots as well, including Chief Wahoo, the cartoonish Native American adorning the uniforms of the Cleveland Indians. In 1933, the owner of the Boston Braves changed the nickname of this pro football team to Redskins. The name moved with the team to Washington, DC, in 1937.

Eventually, protests on college campuses helped the public see this cultural appropriation for what it was—racism. The St. John's Redmen became the Red Storm, and the Warriors of Marquette became the Golden Eagles. After approximately 40 years of debate and controversy at the University of Illinois, the school officially retired the chief in 2007. But the Fighting Illini kept their nickname, war chants can still be heard in the stands, and a graphic of the "Chief" survives on T-shirts and other— unofficial—school gear.

CHAPTER
THREE

A TIME TO
SPEAK OUT

Football and other college sports reflect the values of society outside the campus walls. In the South of the early 1900s, state laws put barriers between African Americans and the voting booth. Schools, restaurants, and hotels enforced a rigorous separation of the races. The lynching of black men for crimes real and imagined was a common occurrence.

White men played sports, while a handful of Native Americans—including future Olympic athlete Jim Thorpe of the Carlisle Indian Industrial School—also took part. African Americans largely were not welcome. It was customary for colleges to sit their black players, if they had any, when facing opposing teams that objected to playing against African Americans. This gentlemen's agreement was in force through the 1930s and was not formally challenged by players, students, or coaches until the fall of 1940.

Very few African Americans were accepted into predominantly white colleges, anyway. At the time Jack Trice attended Iowa State, the school had a total black enrollment of 20 students.[1] Black students studied at Yale, Harvard, and other prestigious Ivy League schools. By the late 1930s, some Southern schools also had broken the color line. The University of Tennessee accepted its first black students in 1961. Under court orders, schools in the South were integrating. But Tennessee still had no black players on its athletic teams.

THE WYOMING 14

At college campuses throughout the nation, the 1960s was the era of protest. Students marched to oppose the Vietnam War (1954–1975) and to support civil rights for minorities. In the opinion of some, however, college sports should be off limits to politics and social issues. Football and basketball, according to this view, had nothing to do with advancing racial justice and were not a fit target for demonstrations of any kind. Instead, sports teams provided relief to the social and political storms playing out in the real world. They were an escape, as much to the students and players as to the millions of fans watching on television.

THE ORIGINAL STUDENT-ATHLETE

Paul Robeson was the son of a runaway slave. He won an athletic scholarship in 1915 to Rutgers University in New Jersey. He was only the third African American to attend the school. He never forgot his first day on the Rutgers football field—when his new teammates did their best to punch, kick, and maul him, and otherwise put him out of action permanently.

Robeson went on to better things, including earning the respect of his teammates and opponents. After earning 15 varsity letters and All-America honors, he went on to a long career as an actor, musician, lawyer, and political activist. He was inducted into the College Football Hall of Fame in 1995, almost 20 years after his death.

Protesters and police clash at a Colorado State football game in 1969, two weeks after 14 black players were cut from Wyoming's team.

The conflict over this point played out in 1969 at the University of Wyoming. The Wyoming Cowboys football team was winning that year, having beaten Arizona, the Air Force Academy, Colorado State, and Texas–El Paso (UTEP). Ranked sixteenth in the nation, the Cowboys were scheduled to play against Brigham Young University (BYU) on October 18. The Mormon Church ran BYU, and it had a strict rule against allowing black men to become priests. Fourteen Wyoming players petitioned Coach Lloyd Eaton to wear armbands in silent protest of this racist policy.

The day before the BYU game, the players—wearing their black armbands—met with Eaton to discuss the issue. It was approximately one year after John Carlos and Tommie Smith, two African American track athletes, had raised their fists in protest at an Olympic medal ceremony in Mexico City. Eaton had already reminded the players that he had a strict rule against any demonstrations by his players. He did not want any factions on his team, and he did not want politics disrupting the simple goal of winning football games.

When he was confronted, Eaton abruptly threw all 14 players off the team. Their appeal for reinstatement was denied. Cowboys fans turned out to support the coach,

THE POWER OF COLLEGE SPORTS

In 2015, racial tensions flared at the University of Missouri. There were confrontations between white and black students and protests against the shooting of a black man by police in the town of Ferguson, Missouri.

Approximately 30 African American players on the football team decided to make their feelings publicly known. They were unhappy with the actions of the university president, Tim Wolfe, who seemed to have little to say on the troubles. So they made an announcement. They would not return to the practice field or play any games until Wolfe was out of a job.

The next football game was scheduled for Arrowhead Stadium, the big pro venue in Kansas City, Missouri. If the game were to be forfeited, it would cost the University of Missouri more than $1 million in fees. Two days after the players announced their strike, Wolfe resigned, and the game went on as planned.

who felt satisfaction at his team's blowout victory against BYU. But the team won only one more game that season, and went 1–9 the next year, before Eaton was fired.[2]

Protests against BYU did not stop with the Wyoming 14. In the next month, black players from San Jose State University refused to take the field against the BYU team. The UTEP track team boycotted a meet against BYU in April 1969. Nine years later, the Mormon Church changed its stance and began allowing black men to enter the priesthood.

BEAR BRYANT MAKES A POINT

By the mid-1960s, Northern teams were demanding that Southern opponents end the exclusion of African American players. Southern teams had to agree or forfeit the games. The pressure to integrate, achieved through mandates from the Supreme Court and the federal government, eventually reached the athletic departments. The universities of Alabama and Mississippi were the last holdouts.

Seeing several rival teams with excellent black players on their rosters, Alabama coach Paul "Bear" Bryant believed he had to make a point. In September 1970, Bryant and his Crimson Tide players were preparing for the first game of the season. Alabama was set to host the University of Southern California (USC) Trojans, an integrated team with a number of outstanding African American players.

By 1970, legendary football coach Bear Bryant knew he needed to find a way to convince Alabama supporters that it was time to integrate the Crimson Tide.

The Trojans won the game handily by a score of 42–21. USC fullback Sam Cunningham ran for 135 yards and two touchdowns in his first collegiate game.[3]

Cunningham realized there was something special about this game. Even though he wasn't a starter, he was put in the game early. "What was even more unbelievable is I got the opportunity to carry the ball. Fullbacks in that era did not carry the ball. I can't tell you what was on the coaches' minds that day, but I can tell that I didn't carry the ball very much the rest of that season."[4]

In fact, Bryant had added USC to the Alabama schedule at the last moment. He knew black players showing up his team on its home field would have a certain effect on Alabama fans. Now, with his team thoroughly beaten, he made his way to the USC locker room and offered the Trojan backfield his personal congratulations. That action also had repercussions. Resistance to the recruitment of black players at Alabama ended—which may have been Bryant's purpose all along.

In 1971, John Mitchell became the first black starter on the Alabama team. He played a key role in Alabama's 17–10 victory over USC in Los Angeles, California. With this, the era of segregation of Southern college football teams was history.

A NEW KIND OF PROTEST

Segregation of college sports may have ended in the 1970s. But athletes are still protesting. In October 2016, the ESPN network hosted its popular *College GameDay* show in Madison, Wisconsin, on the campus of the University of Wisconsin. The show always attracts a crowd of raucous fans waving signs and cheering ESPN's hosts and football pundits. On this day, however, a single person stood tall nearby, quietly holding a big sign: "Broke College/Athlete/Anything Helps."[5]

Nigel Hayes was not afraid to speak up or speak out when he played for the Wisconsin Badgers basketball team.

Nigel Hayes, recruited to play basketball out of Whitmer High in Toledo, Ohio, had drawn the words in bright Badger red. According to the NCAA, which set the rules for his scholarship and eligibility at Wisconsin, Hayes was a student-athlete. That meant he played for a scholarship and an allowance intended to cover the cost of attendance, meaning supplies, travel, and other expenses that all college students have to bear.

The NCAA doesn't want any student—of any race—to earn money from sports. No matter how good they are, players cannot sell the rights to their name or image. They cannot sell autographs or hold any kind of job connected to sports. The NCAA holds fast to amateurism; its rule book decrees: "Student-athletes shall be amateurs in an intercollegiate sport, and their participation should be motivated primarily by education . . . student-athletes should be protected from exploitation by professional and commercial enterprises."[6]

But Hayes knew his real worth. He was a star on a team, one of the best players in the Big Ten Conference and the country. His beloved school was bringing in $40 million a year from television contracts, as well as $10 million from Under Armour, an athletic clothing company, for the right to plaster its logo on the uniforms of Wisconsin's sports teams.[7]

Other Big Ten schools were also making a lot of money, as were coaches, administrators, and television networks. There seemed to be quite a bit of money around college sports, but for the players, there were only NCAA rules that restricted their ability to earn.

Jalen Rose, a former Michigan basketball star, observed: "We live in a country that has profited for hundreds of years off the labor of individuals without having to pay for it. So now you come full circle. Which sports are we having this conversation [about amateurs being paid] in? In football and in basketball, predominantly black sports."[9]

Hayes and many others believe student-athletes in this enterprise should not be playing for a meager cost of attendance stipend. They shouldn't be struggling to get by. Although the full scholarships they earn can be valuable down the road, the equation is still so unequal that, in the opinion of many, it has become fundamentally unfair—and the only way to make it fair is to pay the athletes.

DISCUSSION STARTERS

o   What was the effect of the gentlemen's agreement on college football?
o   Should student-athletes have the right to protest, strike, or disrupt games?
o   Should college teams allow company logos on their uniforms?

CHAPTER FOUR

HBCUs

B y the 1970s, integration had come to college sports. The gentlemen's agreement that prevented teams from fielding their black players, if they had any, was history. Universities across the country accepted students and athletes of any color. Federal laws and Supreme Court decisions banned segregation of schools.

African Americans played, and many excelled. Some went professional, and a few landed big contracts to play before millions of fans in stadiums and on TV. But the integration of college sports had other consequences. The effects—for the minority community and for sports—were not all positive.

At the professional level, the famous Negro Leagues that boasted some of the best baseball players in the country disappeared. Among colleges and universities, integration led to a system where whites largely held the power. Most coaches, administrators, athletic directors, and university presidents were white. Minorities served as the labor on the football field and the basketball court. As compensation, they earned the right to room and board and a chance to earn a college degree.

As author Taylor Branch noted in an article about college football he wrote for the *Atlantic*, the system resembled

In 1961, Ernie Davis of Syracuse University became the first black player to win the Heisman Trophy, given to the nation's best college football player.

an old and traditional institution: "To survey the scene—corporations and universities enriching themselves on the backs of uncompensated young men, whose status as 'student-athletes' deprives them of the right to due process guaranteed by the Constitution—is to catch an unmistakable whiff of the plantation."[1] The integration of college sports also had effects on an education system designed to serve the African American community.

THE HBCUs

The tradition of historically black colleges and universities (HBCUs) dates back to before the US Civil War (1861–1865).

Enslaved people and free African Americans were barred from higher education in the South, so colleges opened in the North for educating them. After the war, many more schools for black students, including Florida A&M University and Grambling State University, were founded in the South.

The HBCUs gave many kids from poor backgrounds a route to an education, a career, and success. Competing in football and other sports, the HBCUs also could draw on a huge pool of talented athletes who didn't get a chance to play at segregated, all-white schools. Many HBCU students came from the surrounding city and region. The schools served as social and cultural centers with local

AN HBCU FOOTBALL FIRST

Black colleges picked up the growing sport of football in the early 1890s. The first intercollegiate game among these schools was played in Salisbury, North Carolina, on a snowy December day in 1892, between the Livingstone College Bears and the Biddle University Golden Bulls. The game was played on the front lawn of Livingstone, where the only score was a touchdown (then worth five points) scored by Biddle.

The first HBCU game also saw the first game-changing dispute over a referee's call. Late in the game, when a Livingstone player recovered a fumble and went in for a score, the Biddle team argued the recovery was made out of bounds. By this time, snow was covering up the field markings, and the officials ruled in Biddle's favor. Soon after this contest, Biddle went the way of many other colleges and banned football for the violence that was causing so many serious injuries. Biddle eventually brought football back, and the Livingstone–Biddle contest became an annual event now known as the Commemorative Classic.

roots and connections, playing an important role in the black community.

There were fierce rivalries among the HBCUs in football, and the schools played for their own national championship. Howard University and Talladega College were the winners of the first Sheridan Poll in 1920. Published by the *Pittsburgh Courier*, the poll determined the best black college football team in the nation every year between 1920 and 1980.[2]

Starting in 1978, the Jake Gaither Trophy honored the best black college football player in the country. Gaither was one of many legendary coaches who led HBCU teams to outstanding seasons. Another was Eddie Robinson, the Grambling football coach who racked up 408 wins, the second-best win total in NCAA Division I history.

LOSING TALENT

In the Gaither Trophy's first year, big changes were coming in college football. Southern universities began recruiting black athletes. Their coaches and athletic directors wanted to compete with the big, rich (and integrated) teams up north. Segregation in college sports was ending, more than two decades after the Supreme Court's *Brown v. Board of Education* ruling held segregation to be unconstitutional.

This turned out to be bad news for the HBCUs. At one time, they could recruit from a big pool of African American

Alabama's Bear Bryant, left, and Florida A&M's Jake Gaither, right, receive their awards for major and small college coach of the year in 1961.

talent. At Florida A&M, for example, Gaither had access to plenty of good players coming up in Florida. He didn't even bother to recruit out of state.

But the HBCUs were not adapting to changing times. Their athletic budgets were smaller, their stadiums were smaller, and their facilities were second class. High school football players saw the now-integrated universities as the big time, and they made their decisions accordingly. Exposure in nationally televised games represented their ticket to playing professional sports after college. Football and other sports at HBCUs went into decline as the schools lost good recruits to predominantly white schools. The black communities that surrounded and staffed them—the networks of students, families, and teachers—began to drift apart.

Author William C. Rhoden played football for and graduated from Morgan State, an HBCU in Baltimore, Maryland. In his book *$40 Million Slaves*, he describes the decline of sports at HBCUs: "Having the black athletes close

A VERY DIFFERENT DEAL FOR HBCUs

In many ways, the HBCUs are still at a serious disadvantage in college athletics. One obvious sign of this can be seen in endorsement contracts. For some schools, shoe and apparel companies pay big bucks for coaches and athletes to wear their brands—the University of Texas at Austin, for example, signed a 15-year endorsement deal with Nike for $200 million.

Nike also struck a deal with the Southwestern Athletic Conference (SWAC), which includes ten historically black colleges. The endorsement was not worth quite as much for the SWAC, which was offered 750 T-shirts, 40 footballs, 48 basketballs, two company internships for SWAC athletes, 600 pairs of shoes for each SWAC school, and a $10,000 equipment allowance for SWAC commissioner Duer Sharp.

An editorial in the *HBCU Digest* on the deal said, "There's nothing wrong with Sharp receiving a creative commission on brokering a deal between his conference and the apparel giant. There's nothing wrong with the conference having in-kind sponsorship for shoes, clothing, and equipment. . . . But there is something wrong when Sharp, and other member presidents who may have been privy to this deal, signed off without any consideration for what the schools really could have gotten from Nike or any other apparel maker courting black colleges."[3]

Jerry Rice went from Mississippi Valley State, a historically black school, to the Pro Football Hall of Fame.

to home allowed them to serve as role models for their own families, as well as for the entire community. . . . After integration, however, black athletes began moving across the country in pursuit of their individual athletic destinies . . . and as a result became alienated from their communities."[4]

It all came down to money. HBCU teams rarely made it to national television. The networks saw the potential audience for their games as too small. Advertisers who paid for time during football games would pay less for the spots. It was rare to see Grambling or Alcorn State compete on ESPN, CBS, or any other network.

Conditions at Grambling got so bad that in 2013 the football players went on strike. For one week, they held a boycott of the locker room, practice field, and a regular-season game. Mississippi Valley State, which produced Pro Football Hall of Famer Jerry Rice, had to close its broken-down football stadium. And the HBCU teams are no longer competitive against other Division I programs. Instead, they're blown out in what are sometimes known as guarantee games they play early in the year against much wealthier programs. The big schools agree to the games for easy victories, while the losing schools are guaranteed large payments for taking part.

Starting in the 1970s, young African Americans who excelled at sports had a chance to land a scholarship and attend colleges that, in the past, would have been off-limits. They also had a chance—a very valuable one—to play on a bigger stage. With the growth of televised sports came contracts that provided big budgets to some college athletic departments. That meant better facilities, better equipment, better training, and bigger stadiums. For an athlete with pro-level talent, this top-tier infrastructure meant a better shot at the big leagues.

DISCUSSION STARTERS

- Why did African Americans need separate colleges of their own?
- How did integration of college sports affect athletic programs at HBCUs?
- Why do black high school athletes seek scholarships from wealthier schools?

CHAPTER FIVE

STUDENT OR ATHLETE?

The NCAA promotes the ideal of the student-athlete. In this notion, college players are students first, athletes second. They play for the love of the game. They wear the colors and the uniforms to represent their school. Above all, they're amateurs. They earn nothing for their talent and effort except a scholarship to attend the school.

College sports, by another ideal, is color blind. The NCAA proudly points to the progress college sports have made since the era of Jim Crow and legal segregation. Nowadays everyone has a shot, regardless of his or her race. Even foreigners can come play, work, study, and achieve. There is no favoritism and no prejudice. What's more, everyone has to play by the same rules.

ACADEMIC STANDARDS

Many of these rules cover academics, and they kick in well before a hopeful athlete's first day on a college campus. To be eligible to play for a Division I or II school, high school students must take 16 core courses (English, math, natural or physical science, social science, foreign language, and comparative religion or philosophy). They must also score at least a 2.3 grade point average (GPA) on those courses. Those who cannot make a 2.3 but can keep a 2.0 GPA and complete their core courses become academic redshirts, meaning they can practice with a team for one year but cannot compete.[1]

The NCAA's Proposition 48, passed in 1986, dictates that high school athletes seeking a college scholarship must make a combined 700 on the Scholastic Aptitude Test, or SAT. The maximum score on the SAT at the time was 1600. If students showing promise in football or basketball want an athletic scholarship, according to the NCAA rules, they also have to "successfully complete 10 of the 16 total required core courses before the start of their seventh semester in high school. Seven of the ten courses must be successfully completed in English, math and science."[2]

TAR HEEL TROUBLES

In 2010, the University of North Carolina was hit with a major academic scandal. Investigators discovered the school had given more than 3,000 students, half of them athletes, impermissible academic assistance.[3] Over a period of 18 years, hundreds of courses in the school's Afro-American Studies department were courses on paper only—there were no homework assignments or exams required, nor were there teachers or classes. The only work needed to pass the courses was a research paper, graded by a nonfaculty counselor.

To the NCAA, however, the paper courses were the university's problem. The group concluded there was no actual cheating involved and thus let the Tar Heels off without penalty, claiming that since nonathletes were also taking the fake courses, there was no violation of the rules.

THE ALL-IMPORTANT APR

The NCAA, not the schools, sets these academic standards. Colleges and high schools are supposed to teach the students, keep the records, and report any problems. If there are any slipups or any cheating, the NCAA investigates and hands down punishment. The organization can deny scholarships or end a coach's career. It can sanction an entire athletic program for the academic performance of its athletes.

One example is the important NCAA metric known as APR, or academic progress rate. APR measures the academic success or failure of student-athletes. If a college cannot graduate its players, or if players' grades are too low, the school can incur penalties. In 2013, two years after winning a national championship, that happened to the University of Connecticut men's basketball team. The Huskies were banned from the NCAA tournament that year for their too-low APR.

Universities want players who can pass tests and handle college-level work so they won't run afoul of APR regulations. But passing these academic bars is not always easy for students from underfunded, poorly equipped inner-city high schools. If they cannot cut it academically, they might have to settle for a junior college, or juco.

A juco player has even less chance of making the pros than a Division I player. And that leads to a new kind of

Jim Calhoun, center, led UConn to the men's basketball title in 2011, but two years later his team was sidelined for its poor academic performance.

segregation. Author Darcy Frey, in his book *The Last Shot,* explains that, "of the players who have gone to junior colleges since the rule was instituted (they are known as 'Prop 48 casualties'), 9 percent are white, 91 percent black."[4]

NEW ACADEMIC STANDARDS

In the past, academic standards set by the NCAA were easier for college athletes to meet. In 1959, the group decreed that student-athletes had to take 12 credits a semester. In 1965, they needed to have a GPA of at least 1.6.[5] In 1973, the standards got tougher. At the same time, many black kids were showing up on previously all-white college campuses, ready to compete. Segregation in college sports was ending. African Americans made up a growing percentage of team rosters, especially in football and basketball.

Former Temple men's basketball coach John Chaney has been an outspoken critic of the NCAA.

Meanwhile, there were calls for stricter NCAA eligibility rules. People said it should no longer be good enough for athletes to be good at sports. They had to be at least C-average students as well.

To some coaches, stricter academic standards looked like an attempt to keep African Americans out of Division I sports. Why were there much easier academic standards set down by the NCAA when most college athletes were white? Why did these standards not apply to

Division III schools, which had the least to offer in terms of scholarships and athletic facilities?

"The NCAA is a racist organization of the highest order," said John Chaney, former basketball coach at Temple University. "I wonder what message they are sending. It's another hardship for black kids made by white folk."[6]

For the schools and the coaches, there is money on the line. The pressure to win at all costs is high. In order to adhere to NCAA guidelines, students and coaches cut corners. Some of the most prestigious and successful NCAA member schools have been caught bending the rules to land recruits or even outright cheating to keep them eligible.

GOPHER PROBLEMS

Clem Haskins went to the segregated Durham High School in Campbellsville, Kentucky, in the early 1960s. He transferred to Taylor County High, becoming the first black student at that school. A standout basketball player, Haskins was recruited by Western Kentucky University, where he and Dwight Smith became the team's first African American players.

Haskins won All-American honors in 1967. After helping the Hilltoppers to three winning seasons and two NCAA tournament appearances, he played nine years in the National Basketball Association (NBA). After retiring from the

Clem Haskins was the national coach of the year in 1997, but two years later he lost his job after an academic scandal rocked the Minnesota basketball program.

pros, Haskins became the first black coach of a mostly white, Southern Division I school: Western Kentucky.

In 1986, the University of Minnesota hired Haskins to coach the men's basketball team. The school had been through numerous scandals. Three Minnesota players, all African Americans from other states, were arrested for rape in Madison. The players were tried and acquitted, but Coach Jim Dutcher resigned in protest after the university suspended the accused players. The Gophers also had the lowest graduation rate in the Big Ten conference.[7] The university turned to Haskins to help clean up the program. He was the first black head coach in school history.

The Gophers improved quickly. In Haskins's third season, they won two games in the NCAA tournament. The next year they made it to the regional final, one game away from the Final Four. Then in 1996–97, the Gophers won a school-record 31 games. They went to the Final Four of the NCAA tournament, and Haskins won many national Coach of the Year awards.

In March 1999, the Gophers were headed for another March Madness appearance. The seedings had them starting in the first round against Gonzaga University. But on the night before that first game, the Saint Paul *Pioneer Press* broke a story that derailed the Gophers and ended Haskins's coaching career.

An academic counselor for the team, Jan Gangelhoff, claimed she had completed more than 400 papers, assignments, and tests for Gophers players during Haskins's time as coach. The team had paid her for the work. The Gophers immediately suspended four players for cheating, just before the Gonzaga game. Then they lost the game.

The university banned itself from postseason play for the 1999–2000 season. It also surrendered 11 scholarships over a five-year period. The university bought out Haskins's coaching contract for $1.5 million. Then it sued to take back the money as punishment for Haskins lying during the cheating investigation. A judge awarded the university $815,000.[8]

GRADING THE NCAA

Minnesota was not the first or last school to go through a cheating scandal. At many colleges and universities, the NCAA student-athlete ideal is not reality. Their college athletes are not playing for the love of the game and the school. Instead, they serve as walking billboards for an athletic program. They generate a mountain of

PILING ON THE PENALTIES

In the University of Minnesota cheating scandal, the school passed down some harsh punishments on itself, on the basketball team, and on Clem Haskins. It was not enough for the NCAA, which piled on with punishments of its own. The team was banned from hanging any championship banners in its arena or mentioning tournament wins in its recruiting brochures. A "show cause" order on Haskins meant there could be penalties on a different school that decided to hire him as a coach. This ended Haskins's coaching career.

The Big Ten also stepped in to cancel Minnesota's conference title, while the NCAA decreed that all Gopher games between 1993 and 1999, as well as its tournament wins, were now off the team's record. Officially, the Gopher men's basketball team is now 0–0 over those years.

money for schools, administrators, and coaches. Their work in the classroom earns the schools nothing beyond keeping them eligible to compete.

As a result, the schools and their teams will overlook, or work around, the NCAA's rule book. Student-athletes not really prepared for college are assisted through course work by coaches and hired tutors. Their scholarships don't necessarily ensure they will be educated or ready for work after college. This is bad news for students already facing barriers due to their background, their experience, or the color of their skin. Many believe it would be better for schools to award scholarships to scholars, pay athletes in the major sports, and put an end to the student-athlete charade.

DISCUSSION STARTERS

- Why are a high schooler's good grades important to the NCAA?
- How much help do you think an athletic department should give to a student-athlete for his or her course work?
- Should athletes earning money for their schools have to attend classes?

CHAPTER SIX

WHERE'S THE MONEY?

To many young black students, the system must appear to be rigged, and not in their favor. They do not see many black people succeeding outside of the sports and entertainment industries. If their families are struggling, they may see limited options for success. They may join the military or go into law enforcement. Going through the education system to land a good job may not be an option.

If they have some athletic talent, they may have a bigger dream: a pro career in basketball, football, or another team sport. Dr. Billy C. Hawkins, a professor at the University of Houston and the author of *The New Plantation*, recalls his own attitude toward the future as a young man:

> *It was seven of us that hung tight. . . . We lived in intensely racially segregated communities. We accepted this racial social ordering and sought to overcome it through sport, or to remain unconscious of it through our perpetual occupation with playing sport. . . . At the age of 14, our small worlds were a playground and most of our waking moments were consumed with some type of athletic activity: after school*

or on the weekends. We did not hang out at the library.[1]

For students of all races, college is expensive. For many, it's out of reach altogether. Grants, scholarships, loans, and earnings from work don't even come close to meeting the cost. For African Americans who don't see a great career looming after high school, an athletic scholarship holds promises and rewards.

So instead of studying, they practice. If they're good enough to win a scholarship, they may be on the road to sports fame and fortune. They have to keep their grades in mind and get a decent SAT score. They know that if they don't qualify for a Division I school, they don't have much chance of going pro.

ONE AND DONE

The NBA passed its "one and done" eligibility rule after several high school graduates turned pro without spending any time in college. Some of these players, such as Kevin Garnett and Kobe Bryant, were spectacularly gifted athletes who were ready for the pros. Others—many others— washed out of the league, costly disappointments to their teams.

"One and done" was meant to prevent the failure of younger NBA rookies. But to many observers, the rule seems unfair. The rule sets the minimum age for players to enter the NBA draft at 19, or at least one year out of high school. That means an 18-year-old good enough to play in the NBA misses the chance to play one year in the league. He also loses out on a year of the NBA's minimum salary, which in 2018 for a first-round pick was more than $1.3 million.[2]

LIFE ON CAMPUS

But an athletic scholarship does not solve every problem. Black kids on campus can have a tough time adjusting. They are out of their neighborhoods and away from their families, maybe for the first time in their lives. They're most often a minority on a predominantly white college campus, and they see few other students like themselves. Culture, language, and manners are different. Isolation and alienation set in.

Rather than fitting in, they stick out. They are curiosities, and if they're on scholarship, they may feel valued only for their athletic talent. Other students may resent the "free ride" the school offers athletes. Why does a great student who doesn't happen to be very good at basketball have to pay for everything? When 58 percent of football and basketball scholarship athletes at Division I schools are African American, it becomes a racial issue.[3] Many college athletes retreat into a small circle of friends and coaches, all associated with their team.

Within that circle, athletes don't have a lot of free time or freedom in general. Academic advisors tell them which courses to take. Many coaches let them know their first priority is to perform on the court or field, paying lip service to academics. They hand down the rules and the schedule: what time to show up for practice, when to be in the weight room, when to show up for tutoring sessions, and when they have to be back in their rooms to meet curfew.

One study of black college athletes found that "being an athlete had forced more blacks into taking a less demanding major, cheating academically, taking [easy] classes, hustling professors for grades, having others write their papers, and taking fewer courses during the term. Blacks felt more pressure to be an athlete first and a student second."[4]

SHOWING THE MONEY

"Amateur competition is a bedrock principle of college athletics," declares the NCAA on its website. "In the collegiate model of sports, the young men and women

HOPE AGAINST HOPE

Most college athletes dream of going pro. Competing in the sport they love and making money—sometimes a lot of it—would make all the hard work, the practices, the injuries, and the tough losses worthwhile.

Many also believe they have a shot. According to one survey, more than three-quarters of all Division I college basketball players believe it's "somewhat likely" that they'll be drafted into a professional league. After all, they have already beaten the odds: approximately 3 percent of all high school basketball players (boys and girls) go on to play in college.

Coaches who recruit young players often emphasize the possibility of going pro to attract the most talented athletes to their schools. But the real chances of a college athlete becoming a professional athlete are slim. In men's basketball it's 1.2 percent; in football it's 1.6 percent; in soccer it's 1.9 percent; in baseball it's 9.4 percent; and in ice hockey it's 0.8 percent.[5]

The annual men's basketball championships—also known as "March Madness"—are a huge moneymaker for the NCAA.

competing on the field or court are students first, athletes second."[6] In the view of NCAA officials, all the rules restricting a college athlete's ability to earn money flow from this principle. Bending the rules would mean violating the principle and degrading what should be the goal of all students: academic achievement.

Although they're amateurs playing for the love of the game, scholarship athletes are in a money business. The school may be earning millions from television contracts.

Regular-season games bring in major money, and tournament appearances even more.

By 2024, March Madness will be worth more than $1 billion a year to the NCAA.[7] There's a lot at stake for schools, coaches, and players. But in this business, the athletes do not play on a level playing field. Coaches and athletic departments have all the power in the relationship. The coach can play or bench the athlete. Players can be suspended or dismissed without cause. The NCAA can ban them for breaking a rule, and there are many rules. Losing a scholarship, or even losing playing time, can cut an athlete's shot at the pros to zero. For many African American students from poor families, losing a scholarship also means an end to any chance at a college degree.

No matter how good they are, student-athletes have no right—according to NCAA rules—to be represented by a union, an agent, or an attorney. They have no power to negotiate the terms of their deal with the school to better advantage. The schools, in turn, deny that the athletes are employees, a status that would give them the right to collective bargaining to address wages, working hours, health and safety rules, and compensation if they are injured on the job.

Many coaches in these sports earn salaries upward of $1 million a year, while players may not, according to NCAA rules, earn anything more than a scholarship and a stipend to cover the costs of attending the school. Players still end up with a shortfall; top-tier football players had an annual deficit of $3,285 in expenses in 2011–12.[8] That means making up the difference with their own savings, or with loans from friends and family. Loans or gifts from anyone connected with the athletic team, of course, are banned.

This puts a lot of pressure on minority students, many of whom come from poor backgrounds. Many are reminded, by family as well as coaches, that the athletic scholarships they have earned are their only realistic means of attaining a better life and livelihood.

THE ELIGIBILITY RULES

The question of pro eligibility also hangs over college athletes, particularly those in basketball, football, hockey, and baseball. When can students make the jump to the pros, and how do they prepare? There are different rules enforced by the NCAA and the pro leagues. The NBA, for example, allows a "one and done" player to enter the draft after a single year of college. The National Football League (NFL) demands that draft candidates be three years out of high school. Arguments for eligibility rules often center on the value of an education and the risk to younger players of injury at the pro levels. But these rules, in the view of many, deny talented players the chance to earn a living.

There is another issue when players, many of them black and Hispanic, are from poor backgrounds—the wait for eligibility means a roadblock to their opportunity. It means risking an injury at the college level that can end their pro career before it even starts. It also brings about under-the-table transactions and deals that break NCAA rules. If students are caught receiving illegal payments, they can end up banned from competition, and that can mean saying goodbye to a professional sports career.

DISCUSSION STARTERS

- The NCAA claims it wants its student-athletes to remain amateurs so they can focus on academics. Can you think of any other reasons the NCAA would mandate amateurism?
- Do you think the "one and done" rule is fair to skilled basketball players who are ready for the pros?

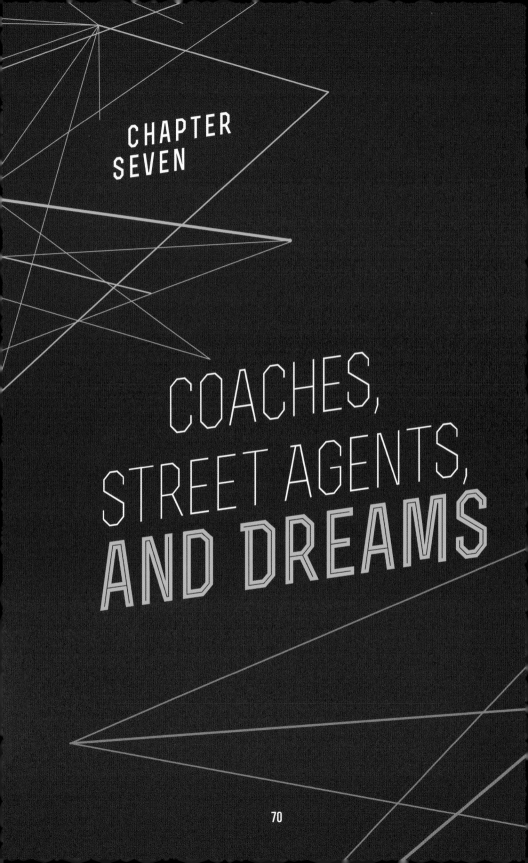

CHAPTER
SEVEN

COACHES, STREET AGENTS, AND DREAMS

M any skilled high school athletes may see a four-year
scholarship, or a pro sports contract, as a means of
rising out of poverty. It doesn't matter that the school may
be thousands of miles away from their homes, families, and
neighborhoods. The appeal of a career doing what they
love, and earning millions for it, draws them into sports such
as basketball and football, the "money sports" at the college
level. Their families may pin their hopes on the chances of a
talented son or daughter reaching the big time or being the
first in the family with a college degree.

Among college coaches, competition is fierce for
talented prospects. The recruiting begins with letters to
high school coaches and visits to school gyms. It continues
at summer sports camps, where coaches watch attentively
in the stands, then make short conversation with the
players. NCAA rules prohibit any prolonged contact
between recruiting coaches and players. Among the
coaches, competition is fierce for the best players.

A middleman gets involved, often exploiting both sides
in the process. Sometimes referred to as street agents,
they serve as go-betweens for the coaches, who are under
strict NCAA rules about direct contact with high school
athletes. The hoped-for reward for street agents is a player

who will eventually hire them as a real agent when they become pros.

A spot on a Division I team is the dream of most high school basketball players. That four-year college degree could mean a good job and better circumstances after college. For those who struggle in class, the athletic scholarship also may represent the only chance they do have of getting into college.

A CHANGE OF HEART

The NCAA has a response to critics of its amateurism model. The organization believes that barring college athletes from earning money upholds the idea that academics always come first. After all, student-athletes at many colleges earn full scholarships, and with those scholarships they have the chance to earn a college degree—the ticket, for many, to a successful professional career after graduation.

Walter Byers, executive director of the NCAA from 1951 to 1988, was partly responsible for creating the student-athlete ideal and the NCAA's rules on amateurism. Toward the end of his life, Byers looked back on his work and found that somehow it had all gone wrong. The enormous amount of money involved in televised sports, in Byers's view, was corrupting the process and cheating the players.

Long after he retired, Byers was given an award for his lifelong contribution to amateur sports. In his acceptance speech, he nearly turned it down. "Each generation of young persons come along and all they ask is 'Coach, give me a chance, I can do it.' And it's a disservice to these young people that the management of intercollegiate athletics stays in place committed to an outmoded code of amateurism. And I attribute that to, quite frankly, to the neo-plantation mentality that exists on the campuses of our country and in the conference offices and in the NCAA, [where] the coach owns the athlete's feet, and the college owns the athlete's body."[1]

THE FIRST-GENS

For black families who experienced segregation for generations, a son or daughter winning a scholarship meant that, possibly for the first time, a member of the family was getting a higher education. But the percentage of scholarship winners who are the first generation in their family to attend college—the "first-gens"—is falling.

By 2015, the percentage of Division I athletes who were first-gens stood at 14.2 percent, while among all freshmen at four-year colleges the percentage of first-gens was actually higher, at 17.2 percent. "That's because we're picking kids from families with collegiate backgrounds," explains E. D'Wayne Robinson of Coppin State University. "We are more careful now about who we take. Our jobs are on the line. It's all about winning and losing—and APR. More about the APR."[2]

An opposite trend is taking place at HBCUs, where first-gens are increasing. These schools are at a disadvantage, as they don't get the television revenue that pays for better facilities and bigger coaching staffs. Families that have spent a lot of money on training, equipment, summer camps, and the like are less likely to accept a scholarship from a second-tier school that cannot compete on the field. The result is economic segregation of colleges—a reminder, in money terms, of the segregation enforced by law in the past.

More first-generation students are graduating from HBCUs than ever before.

HITTING THE SHOT

Seeing his image, his left-handed shot, his height, and his jersey number on a player in a video game in 2009, Ed O'Bannon knew he had been programmed into the game in all but name. Unfortunately, Electronic Arts (EA), the company that designed the game, had not bothered to ask his permission. And by NCAA rules, the University of California, Los Angeles (UCLA) star couldn't do a thing about it.

The NCAA does not allow its athletes to earn money from their own names or likenesses. Instead, licensing fees go to the NCAA. Not happy with the arrangement, O'Bannon sued. Known simply as the "O'Bannon case" to anyone who deals with the NCAA, the issue was partially settled in 2014, when EA agreed to pay damages of $40 million to college football and basketball players who had been used by the company in its games without permission.[3]

SOMETHING NEW

Writers and observers see economic inequality in the money sports and point out that it might be fair to just pay the players what they're worth to the schools. The NCAA stands in the way with several arguments. Not all schools can afford to pay athletes; those that cannot will fall behind, and competition will suffer. Paying salaries to the best players, and nothing

HBCUs AND THE NFL

In the late 1950s, very few African American college players were going on to play in the NFL. The professional teams had little interest in drafting players out of HBCU teams, which they considered second rate. Or they may simply have held to traditional notions of separating the races on the playing field.

Things changed quickly when the American Football League (AFL) started up in 1960. The AFL was a direct competitor to the NFL, and it had to get its players from anywhere it could, including the HBCUs. With this new crop of talent, the upstart league began challenging the NFL for dominance. After AFL teams won a couple of Super Bowls, NFL teams reconsidered. More NFL teams began drafting African American players, and the two leagues completed a merger in 1970.

to others, will cause further injustice, resentment, and legal issues. Players aren't mature enough to negotiate contracts. Athletic salaries will interfere with their education.

Andy Schwarz believes he has a better way. He's a lawyer who has been working on NCAA cases for many years. Like many others, he sees college sports as an unfair transfer of great wealth from players to coaches and administrators, from largely black to mostly white. He believes college players should be paid. Unlike many others, however, he has come up with a plan to do it. "Litigation hasn't worked," says Schwarz. "Organization hasn't worked. Legislation, there's no way it's going to work. . . . The only thing that was really left was competition."[4]

The first step relies on the separateness of historically black colleges and universities. The HBCUs would form an entirely new conference and would be allowed to pay their players. The players could also earn money by selling autographs or allowing their names and images on products and school merchandise. They could hire agents. They could declare themselves eligible for the pros. Being drafted would not end their eligibility to play for a college team.

Schwarz believes the lure of earning what they are worth would appeal to athletes who feel the current system takes advantage of their talents—in effect, gets their labor free. As a result, the "pay for play" conference would begin

Former UCLA star Ed O'Bannon went to court to fight for the rights of college athletes to be reimbursed when their images are used in video games.

to draw athletic talent away from the NCAA members. Instead of going to Ohio State or Duke to play for the love of the game, for example, a solid football or basketball player could attend an HBCU and make good money from the day he arrives on campus. There would be no scholarships— those would go to the scholars.

Schwarz's new conference will need money to get off the ground. The biggest expense would be setting up a fund to pay salaries in the early years. As long as the new league cannot compete with NCAA teams, it will have a tough time signing TV contracts and becoming financially viable. The money will have to come from elsewhere.

Schwarz has considered asking for seed money from NBA megastar LeBron James and Mark Cuban, the billionaire owner of the Dallas Mavericks. Cuban has a reputation for disrupting old business models and creating new ones. "One of the ways to bust up a monopoly is through disruption," Schwarz says. "That's the idea here."[5]

Of course, the NCAA can fight back. It would likely disqualify the HBCU teams from competing against teams that remain within the NCAA. The HBCU teams and their paid players would be shut out of the March Madness tournament as well as the annual college football playoff. The NCAA also could disqualify other HBCU athletic programs—even if their athletes were unpaid—from NCAA competition.

Schwarz and his partners, all trained lawyers, are prepared. Their business plan finishes with this statement: "If the NCAA boycotted the HBCU's non-basketball programs, simply because the HBCUs chose to pay their basketball athletes, this would make for a sympathetic lawsuit of David vs. Goliath."[6]

DISCUSSION STARTERS

- Why do you think it is important for colleges to accept first-gen students?
- Do you think colleges and universities should pay their athletes?
- If you were a high school athlete, would a college scholarship be enough reward for the many years of hard work and practice it takes to make it to the college level?

CHAPTER EIGHT

UPHILL BATTLES IN WOMEN'S BASKETBALL

Lusia Harris grew up playing and winning at basketball. She was tall, strong, tough, and smart, and she had a solid jump shot. But in the 1960s, an African American girl in a small Mississippi town did not have many options when it came to sports. As her high school graduation approached, she prepared for college at Alcorn State, a historically black school up the road in Claiborne County.

Before signing the enrollment papers, however, Harris got a visit from Melvin Hemphill, an admissions counselor from Delta State. The school in Cleveland, Mississippi, was even closer to her hometown of Minter City. Hemphill explained the reason for his visit: Delta State was starting a women's basketball program, and he wanted Harris on the team.

She agreed. For four years, Harris was the only African American player on the team. "It wasn't very nice there," she recalled. "I came from an all-black school—all-black high school, and there weren't many black students and no black teachers."[1] Nevertheless, she led little Delta State, with its brand-new women's basketball team, to a record of 109–6 and three national championships over four seasons.

CAREER OVER

Harris starred for Team USA in the 1976 Summer Olympics, the first to include women's basketball as a sport. After that experience, Harris played for the Houston Angels in the Women's Basketball League. The team disbanded in 1980, ending her playing career. She worked at Delta State as an admissions counselor and spent four years as an assistant basketball coach. When the head coach retired, she was not even considered as a replacement.

Instead, Harris went to a head coaching job at Texas Southern, a school in Houston. She struggled with a small budget and low respect from the school's administrators. After two years, she was fired. Her marriage broke up, and she suffered a nervous breakdown. Her life in basketball was over.

Harris was given a place in the National Basketball Hall of Fame and the Women's Basketball Hall of Fame. But among even professional women players, she is largely forgotten, even though she did a lot to put women's

OLYMPIC MATCHUPS

Harris played a key role in bringing the United States basketball glory at the 1976 Olympics in Montreal, Canada. Playing center, she scored the first points ever in Olympic women's basketball history. She also led the US squad, which finished with a silver medal, with 15 points and 7 rebounds per game.[2] But even Harris could not quite match up with towering, 6-foot-11 center Uljana Semjonova of the Soviet Union. The gold-medal game went to the Soviets by a lopsided score of 112–77.

Despite leading Delta State to the 1977 national championship, Harris, with ball, is not a household name, even among women's basketball fans.

basketball into the spotlight. Author William C. Rhoden, in his book *$40 Million Slaves*, had a theory: "Harris's invisibility is a symbol of the race-tinged ambivalence African American women encounter within the women's sports movement. It's often been noted that women of color in sports have been rendered nearly invisible, a reflection of America's lingering association of femininity with whiteness."[3]

For women's college sports, things changed after Title IX. This was the rule that required universities to give adequate resources and facilities to women's athletics. After Title IX was passed, female athletes and their teams emerged as stars. This was also the era when segregation in sports largely disappeared. The circumstances were set for the rise of a women's sports star, and Rebecca Lobo took center stage.

THE LOBO EFFECT

For the Huskies of the University of Connecticut (UConn), this would be a game like no other. It was January 16, 1995. For the first time ever, the Huskies were facing the Lady Vols of Tennessee—a women's basketball powerhouse. As usual, the Lady Vols had the best talent in the country, and they had a legend on the bench in coach Pat Summitt, who had played on the 1976 Olympic team with Harris. The Lady Vols were the top-ranked team in the nation.

Now they were up against second-ranked UConn and star forward Rebecca Lobo.

CONNECTICUT AND ESPN

Lobo's Connecticut Huskies benefited from a very good neighbor down the road. The ESPN network, based in Bristol, Connecticut, was growing a national television audience. The network carried near-daily broadcasts of men's college games through the basketball season. When it found a star and a championship team in its back yard, its coverage of women's basketball increased.

The network now carries women's basketball all season and broadcasts the NCAA women's tournament at the same time as March Madness. In the meantime, the Connecticut women's team won ten NCAA championships between 2000 and 2016, and coach Geno Auriemma has racked up more than 1,000 victories.

She was a Cuban American senior from Southwick, Massachusetts. At six feet four inches, Lobo towered over most opponents. Quick for her height, she could shoot, pass, and outrebound anybody on the court.

The game was carried on national television and attracted a sold-out crowd to Gampel Pavilion on the UConn campus. Lobo led the Huskies to a convincing 77–66 win, putting the Connecticut program and women's basketball on the map for good.

MAKING A STAR

Growing up, Lobo knew she wanted to play basketball, and she had the attention of college recruiters. Summitt, among others, would have been glad to have her. But Lobo chose Connecticut for its coach, Geno Auriemma. "Coach Auriemma was the person I wanted to play for above all others," she later told an interviewer.[4] Connecticut had a good but not great team and was not yet a national power. Lobo made the Huskies great, and ever since that 1995 championship game, Connecticut has been the best women's college basketball program in the country.

After college, Lobo led the US women's team to an Olympic gold medal in 1996. She then became a star in the Women's National Basketball Association (WNBA), the pro women's basketball league founded in 1997. She was a role model for young players in high school, who—simply

Cuban American basketball star Rebecca Lobo helped the University of Connecticut win its first national championship in 1995.

because of their gender or their ethnic background—had not thought much about making a living at basketball. She helped create a new generation of Hispanic players and fans who followed her games at UConn and then with the Houston Comets. "I remember . . . playing a game in Los Angeles. There was a whole section in the Staples Center filled with Hispanic boys and girls who came to cheer me on. Pretty amazing."[5]

When Lobo was at UConn, Hispanic athletes were still hard to find in the money sports. Financial barriers prevented many families from sending their kids to college or signing them up for summer leagues and amateur teams. A few sports, including volleyball, water polo, and soccer, had a good number of Hispanic players. In football,

AVOIDING SPORTS

There are not many Hispanic girls taking part in sports at the college level. The reasons lie, at least partially, in Latino culture and traditions. Julio Pabón, who runs a sports marketing agency in New York City, explained to a newspaper reporter that, "in the Latino community especially, girls have to be home. If you have three siblings in the house all about the same ages, 17, 16, 14, the girl is doing more chores than the guys."[6] It's also typical for teenagers in these families to take part-time jobs or care for younger siblings to help the family. That makes it tough to make time for sports.

The lack of role models may also be a factor. There aren't many famous Hispanic women in sports for young Latinas to follow, while the entertainment business has Jennifer Lopez, Selena Gomez, and Michelle Rodriguez, among others. Hispanic girls are still waiting for their own version of Serena Williams, the African American tennis player, to emerge as a superstar professional athlete.

most were kickers, with almost none at the key position of quarterback. Basketball, both men's and women's, had very few Hispanic stars—with the exception of Lobo. The disparity persists, with Hispanics underrepresented in most college athletics. The roots lie more in economics and culture rather than in segregation or racism.

Despite aspects of racial inequality hanging over college sports, black athletes have some historic and cultural benefits that have been denied to Hispanics. A network of black colleges have been recruiting athletes for a century, and these schools were pioneers in the racial integration of American sports. There has never been such a network for Latinos, who now make up 17 percent of the US population.

In Latin America, baseball has long been a popular sport. Players of all ages and skill levels take part, and Hispanics are well represented at the college and professional level. But they make up a small percentage in other sports, and they win a very small percentage of athletic scholarships. Among college populations overall, Hispanics made up 12 percent of the students but only 4 percent of the scholarship athletes.[7]

Financial considerations are on the short list of causes. Sports such as tennis and hockey, in which equipment and training are more expensive, effectively shut out minorities from lower-income households. In addition, there is a lack of pro opportunity and financial reward in certain sports where the Hispanic population is higher: volleyball, soccer, track and field, and water polo. A language barrier and cultural pressures to work to support a family, rather than attend higher education, may also contribute to the absence of Hispanic players from college teams.

DISCUSSION STARTERS

- Why did Rebecca Lobo want to go to the University of Connecticut, which was not a women's basketball power at the time?
- What family traditions have stopped Hispanic girls from going out for sports?
- Why has women's basketball, at the college level, become so popular?

CHAPTER
NINE

THE LEADERSHIP
GAP

It was seven in the morning, and Will Robinson was ready. He had been playing golf since the age of 12, when he started working at an Ohio country club as a caddie. Now he was captain of his high school team, playing on the big stage: the Ohio state high school golf tournament in Columbus.

Not many golfers matched up with Robinson as an athlete. He had earned varsity letters in football, golf, basketball, baseball, and track. At this particular tournament, however, Robinson would be walking the course, and playing, by himself. He was black, and in the 1920s, course rules banned him from joining the white golfers.

No matter. Robinson finished second overall. He went on to big things in basketball as well. In 1970, Illinois State hired him as the first black head coach in NCAA Division I history. In five years with the Redbirds, Robinson finished with a 78–51 overall record and never had a losing season.

Down in Louisiana, Eddie Robinson (no relation to Will) was piling up even better numbers. The head football coach of the feared Grambling Tigers, Robinson led the team to 17 conference titles and seven National Negro championships. He ended with a career record of 408 wins, 165 losses, and

Will Robinson, right, *greets former NBA star Isiah Thomas in 2005.*

15 ties. That made him second only to John Gagliardi of Minnesota's St. John's University in all-time football wins.

By the mid-1970s, however, Grambling and other black colleges were losing good recruits to integrating white schools. The heyday of the Tigers was passing, even with Eddie Robinson on the sidelines. Many black players were showing up on the rosters of the big schools, even though the coaches and athletic department administrators at these schools were almost all white.

THE COLOR LINE

When laws or customs separate the races, a "color line" exists. A color line still exists in college sports. The barrier holding back African Americans and other minorities has disappeared on the football field and the basketball court, but it remains in place on the sidelines and in the offices where important decisions are made. It is still present in the highest level of college football. As of 2017, 86.7 percent of all athletic directors among those top-level schools were white—but 56 percent of the players at these same schools were black.[1]

University athletic directors are responsible for personnel decisions in the athletic department. They hire and fire coaches. They deal with college presidents and the boards of regents that run the schools. They meet with alumni and board members, oversee fundraising, draw up budgets, sign television contracts, and try to keep the program in compliance with NCAA regulations. They're important people because athletics at many schools are a key source of income. They're hired and fired, in turn, by university presidents.

There are no longer rules about what race the athletic director or the president at a college needs to be. That would be against federal and state laws. There might no longer be unwritten rules or "gentlemen's agreements" either. But there are habits.

COLOR TRENDS

People making a hiring decision tend to hire someone who looks like them—someone with a similar background, experience, and way of speaking. With a common background, after all, it should be easier to understand each other and work together. For that reason, college presidents and athletic directors still have a habit of not hiring minorities.

That may also be the reason that presidents of the NCAA have always been white men—there has never been a woman or a minority at the organization's head. The same thing has happened among the "power five" conferences—the Atlantic Coast Conference, Big Ten, Big 12, Pac-12, and SEC. Every conference commissioner in these leagues has been a white man. And as of 2017, only seven of the 65 "power five" schools had a black head football coach.[3]

When the schools do search for a new coach, they hire head-hunting firms—all having white presidents—to

Carla Williams meets with the media after being hired as the athletic director at the University of Virginia in 2017.

help find good candidates. Writing in the *Washington Post*, reporter Adam Kilgore explains, "While those in charge may not be actively blocking black coaches, they most likely rely on established relationships for key hires. And the likelihood will be the people they are closest to, both professionally and socially, will look like them."[4]

OREGON CHANGES THE RULES

In the past, state and federal legislatures wrote laws to right old wrongs. After the Civil War, changes were made to the US Constitution to give people who had been enslaved equal legal standing as citizens, at least in theory. Laws passed in the middle of the 1900s ended Jim Crow statutes and regulations in states that still had them on the books.

When it comes to coaching and administrative jobs, the state of Oregon followed this example. In 2009, the state passed House Bill 3118. According to the text of the bill, schools receiving funds from the state must "interview one or more qualified minority applicants when hiring a head coach or athletic director, unless the institution was unable to identify a qualified minority applicant who was willing to interview for the position."[5]

Among the 50 states, Oregon stands alone in putting the so-called Eddie Robinson Rule into law. After the law passed, Portland State hired Valerie Cleary, an African American woman, as its athletic director. Two days later, the University of Oregon hired Willie Taggart, also an African

BREAKING THROUGH

Although there are few black or Hispanic men in the job of athletic director, women started breaking through in 2016 and 2017. Mary Ellen Gillespie (University of Hartford), Mary Tuite (San Jose State), and Donna Woodruff (Loyola Maryland) all were hired as athletic directors in that span. In September 2017, Carla Williams at the University of Virginia became the first African American woman to be hired as an athletic director among the "power five" conferences.

Willie Taggart took over the Oregon football program in 2017.

American, to lead its successful football program. What happened? What persuaded Oregon to pass its law?

While a student at Portland State, Sam Sachs got involved in the search for a new football coach. Sachs asked the school administrators to interview a minority candidate. Instead, the school hired former NFL head coach Jerry Glanville. Over three years, Glanville ran up a 9–24 win-loss record. After the 2009 season, he was fired.

Once again, it was time to look for a new coach, and this time a new state law was in effect. Sachs had played an important role in lobbying the state legislature to pass the bill. The law did not force the hiring of a black coach—it only required schools to interview a minority candidate. There were no penalties enforced for violating or ignoring the law. "My goal wasn't to punish schools," said Sachs. "My goal was to get schools to think differently and act differently. And that's what's happened."[6]

There are still barriers and inequality in college sports. But the actions of determined individuals can overcome the color lines. Nigel Hayes and Sam Sachs are examples, while the life stories of Sam Cunningham, Rebecca Lobo, Jack Trice, and other trailblazers like them inspire athletes through their ability and courage. Yet in their dealings with the athletes who play the games, the NCAA and college athletic departments still face questions of fundamental fairness and economic justice.

DISCUSSION STARTERS

- Why is there still a color line in college sports?
- What is the best way to bring minority coaches equal opportunity?
- Is it a good idea for state laws to force schools to interview a minority candidate?

ESSENTIAL FACTS

SIGNIFICANT EVENTS

- In 1970, USC trounces Alabama in an early-season football game, turning the tide on segregation in the Southeastern Conference (SEC).

- In 1986, the NCAA passes Proposition 48, requiring minimum grade point averages and SAT scores for incoming college athletes.

- In 2010, the NCAA signs a 14-year, $10.8 billion deal to televise the March Madness basketball tournament.

KEY PLAYERS

- Walter Byers served as the executive director of the NCAA from 1951 to 1981, and he was the originator of the NCAA's rules on student-athletes and amateurism.

- Ed O'Bannon, a former UCLA player, sued for the right to earn royalties from the use of his name and likeness, a case that challenged the NCAA's total control of student-athletes' financial rights.

- Eddie Robinson coached the Grambling Tigers, a football powerhouse among historically black colleges and universities, for more than 50 years.

- Head coach Don Haskins and the Texas Western men's basketball team made history in 1966 as the first to start five African American players in the NCAA title game.

IMPACT ON SOCIETY

College sports have become a multibillion-dollar entertainment industry. Although athletic teams no longer segregate minority and white players, inequalities persist and prevent athletes from earning what many say they are worth to their schools.

QUOTE

"I wasn't out to be a pioneer when we played Kentucky. I was simply playing the best players on the team, and they happened to be black."

—*Coach Don Haskins, Texas Western College*

GLOSSARY

color line
The barrier, sometimes by law and sometimes by custom, preventing a racial minority from taking part in sports teams, clubs, professions, or facilities limited to whites.

conference
A group of sports teams, usually from a common region, who play against each other during the regular season.

first-gen
A student who is the first in his or her family to attend a college or university.

gentlemen's agreement
An informal and nonbinding arrangement between two or more parties that is enforced by the honor of those agreeing to the parameters rather than any legal stipulations.

grade point average (GPA)
System on a scale of 1 (D) to 4 (A) used by colleges and universities to measure academic progress.

historically black colleges and universities (HBCUs)

Academic institutions founded to educate African Americans, especially where higher education was closed to them based on their race.

injunction

An order from a court meant to stop or prevent an activity found by the court to be unlawful.

integration

The process of making schools, parks, and other facilities available to people of all races on an equal basis.

March Madness

The annual NCAA basketball tournament that is the most important single source of money for many colleges and universities.

mascot

A human or animal representative of a sports team.

plantation

A large farm or estate where crops such as cotton, sugar, and tobacco are grown, usually by laborers who live on the estate.

segregation

The practice of separating groups of people based on race, gender, ethnicity, or other factors.

ADDITIONAL RESOURCES

SELECTED BIBLIOGRAPHY

Frey, Darcy. *The Last Shot: City Streets, Basketball Dreams.* Houghton
    Mifflin, 2004.

Hawkins, Billy C. *The New Plantation: Black Athletes, College Sports, and
    Predominantly White NCAA Institutions.* Palgrave Macmillan, 2013.

King, C. Richard, and Charles Fruehling Springwood. *Beyond the Cheers: Race as
    Spectacle in College Sport.* SUNY, 2001.

Nocera, Joe, and Ben Strauss. *Indentured: The Battle to End the Exploitation of
    College Athletes.* Portfolio, 2018.

Rhoden, William C. *$40 Million Slaves: The Rise, Fall, and Redemption of the Black
    Athlete.* Crown, 2006.

FURTHER READINGS

Abdul-Jabbar, Kareem, and Raymond Obstfeld. *Becoming Kareem: Growing Up
    On and Off the Court.* Little, 2017.

Harris, Duchess, and Jillian C. Wheeler. *Race in Sports Media Coverage.*
    Abdo, 2019.

Zuckerman, Gregory, Elijah Zuckerman, and Gabriel Zuckerman. *Rising
    Above: How 11 Athletes Overcame Challenges in Their Youth to Become Stars.*
    Philomel, 2016.

ONLINE RESOURCES

To learn more about race in college sports, visit **abdobooklinks.com**. These links are routinely monitored and updated to provide the most current information available.

MORE INFORMATION

For more information on this subject, contact or visit the following organizations:

CENTER FOR CIVIL AND HUMAN RIGHTS
100 Ivan Allen Jr. Boulevard
Atlanta, GA 30313
678-999-8990
civilandhumanrights.org

This museum is dedicated to the US civil rights movement and its connection to today's human rights struggles throughout the world.

NCAA HALL OF CHAMPIONS
700 W. Washington Street
Indianapolis, IN 46204
317-916-4255
ncaahallofchampions.org

Interactive exhibits and artifacts bring to life great moments in NCAA history.

SOURCE NOTES

CHAPTER 1. WHITE BALL, BLACK BALL

1. Robyn Norwood. "Don Haskins, 78; Basketball Coach Was First to Win NCAA Title with 5 Black Starters." *Los Angeles Times*, 8 Sept. 2008. latimes.com. Accessed 31 July 2018.

2. Michael K. Bohn. "Texas Western's 1966 Championship Win Changed College Basketball 50 Years Ago." *Oklahoman*, 17 Mar. 2016. newsok.com. Accessed 31 July 2018.

CHAPTER 2. NOT PLAYING FAIR

1. Rodney K. Smith. "A Brief History of the National Collegiate Athletic Association's Role in Regulating Intercollegiate Athletics." *Marquette Sports Law Review*, Volume 11. scholarship.law.marquette.edu. Accessed 31 July 2018.

2. John Rosengren. "A Football Martyr." *SBNation*, 25 Nov. 2014. sbnation.com. Accessed 31 July 2018.

3. C. Richard King and Charles Fruehling Springwood. *Beyond the Cheers: Race as Spectacle in College Sports*. SUNY Press, 2001. 17.

4. King and Fruehling Springwood, *Beyond the Cheers*, 17–18.

CHAPTER 3. A TIME TO SPEAK OUT

1. John Rosengren. "A Football Martyr." *SBNation*, 25 Nov. 2014. sbnation.com. Accessed 31 July 2018.

2. Phil White. "The Black 14: Race, Politics, Religion and Wyoming Football." *WyoHistory.org*, 8 Nov. 2014. wyohistory.org. Accessed 31 July 2018.

3. Zach Helfand. "Separated from the Myths, Sam Cunningham's Story Remains an Inspiration." *Los Angeles Times*, 31 Aug. 2016. latimes.com. Accessed 31 July 2018.

4. Sarah Bergstrom. "Sam 'Bam' Cunningham: The Unlikely Catalyst." *USC Trojans*, 9 Feb. 2016. uscbhm.com. Accessed 31 July 2018.

5. Tom Ziller. "Nigel Hayes Is the Right Athlete to Protest the NCAA." *SBNation*, 17 Oct. 2016. sbnation.com. Accessed 31 July 2018.

6. Johnny Smith. "The Job Is Football: The Myth of the Student-Athlete." *American Historian*, n.d. tah.oah.org. Accessed 31 July 2018.

7. Ziller, "Nigel Hayes Is the Right Athlete to Protest the NCAA."

8. Nigel Hayes. "Don't Just Shut Up and Play." *Players' Tribune*, 10 May 2017. theplayerstribune.com. Accessed 31 July 2018.

9. Sam Amick. "ESPN Analyst Jalen Rose: NCAA System Like 'Indentured Servitude.'" *USA Today*, 27 Feb. 2018. usatoday.com. Accessed 31 July 2018.

CHAPTER 4. HBCUs

1. Reeves Wiedeman. "The End of College Football?" *New Yorker*, 19 Sept. 2011. newyorker.com. Accessed 31 July 2018.

2. "Football Championship Subdivision Records." *NCAA.org*, 2015. fs.ncaa.org. Accessed 31 July 2018.

3. J. L. Carter Sr. "SWAC–Nike Partnership Shows Low Corporate Appeal of HBCU Sports." *HBCU Digest*, 27 Nov. 2015. hbcudigest.com. Accessed 31 July 2018.

4. William C. Rhoden. *$40 Million Slaves: The Rise, Fall, and Redemption of the Black Athlete*. Crown, 2006. 137.

CHAPTER 5. STUDENT OR ATHLETE?

1. Kevin Trahan. "The NCAA's New Academic Redshirt Rule Will Leave Some Recruits Ineligible as Freshmen." *SBNation*, 27 Jan. 2016. sbnation.com. Accessed 31 July 2018.

2. "Academic Standards for Initial-Eligibility." *NCAA.org*, n.d. ncaa.org. Accessed 31 July 2018.

3. Marc Tracy. "NCAA: North Carolina Will Not Be Punished for Academic Scandal." *New York Times*, 13 Oct. 2017. nytimes.com. Accessed 31 July 2018.

4. Darcy Frey. *The Last Shot: City Streets, Basketball Dreams*. Mariner, 2004. 187.

5. Delgreco K. Wilson. "The Black Cager." *DelgrecoWilson.com*, 18 Sept. 2014. delgrecowilson.com. Accessed 31 July 2018.

6. Wilson, "The Black Cager."

7. Jay Weiner. "Fresh Start for Haskins and Minnesota." *New York Times*, 1 Feb. 1987. nytimes.com. Accessed 31 July 2018.

8. "Haskins Must Return $815,000." *Los Angeles Times*, 14 May 2002. latimes.com. Accessed 31 July 2018.

SOURCE NOTES CONTINUED

CHAPTER 6. WHERE'S THE MONEY?

1. Billy Hawkins. *The New Plantation: Black Athletes, College Sports, and Predominantly White NCAA Institutions.* Palgrave Macmillan, 2010. 3.

2. "2018–19 NBA Rookie Scale." *Real GM,* n.d. realgm.com. Accessed 31 July 2018.

3. Shaun R. Harper et al. "Black Male Student-Athletes and Racial Inequities in NCAA Division I College Sports." *University of Pennsylvania Center for the Study of Race and Equity in Education,* 2013. equity.gse.upenn.edu. Accessed 31 July 2018.

4. Hawkins, *The New Plantation,* 129.

5. Jake New. "A Long Shot." *Inside Higher Ed,* 27 Jan. 2015. insidehighered.com. Accessed 31 July 2018.

6. "Amateurism." *NCAA.org,* n.d. ncaa.org. Accessed 31 July 2018.

7. Marc Tracy. "NCAA Extends Basketball Deal with CBS and Turner through 2032." *New York Times,* 13 Apr. 2016. nytimes.com. Accessed 31 July 2018.

8. April Fulton. "Hunger Games: College Athletes Make Play for Collective Bargaining." *National Public Radio,* 21 Apr. 2014. npr.org. Accessed 31 July 2018.

9. Andrew Doughty. "How Much Each NCAA Tournament Team Earned for Their Conference." *Hero Sports,* 17 Mar. 2018. herosports.com. Accessed 31 July 2018.

CHAPTER 7. COACHES, STREET AGENTS, AND DREAMS

1. Karen Given. "Walter Byers: The Man Who Built the NCAA, Then Tried to Tear It Down." *WBUR,* 13 Oct. 2017. wbur.org. Accessed 31 July 2018.

2. Tom Farrey. "The Gentrification of College Hoops." *Undefeated,* 17 Mar. 2017. theundefeated. com. Accessed 31 July 2018.

3. Tom Farrey. "Players, Game Makers Settle for $40M." *ESPN,* 31 May 2014. espn.com. Accessed 31 July 2018.

4. Shira Springer. "HBCUs and Their Role in Disrupting the College Sports 'Cartel.'" *WBUR,* 13 Oct. 2017. wbur.org. Accessed 31 July 2018.

5. Rob Thompson. "This Is How to 'Disrupt' the NCAA and Pay College Basketball Players." *ESPN San Antonio,* 21 June 2017. espnsa.com. Accessed 31 July 2018.

6. Patrick Hruby. "The Plot to Disrupt the NCAA with a Pay-for-Play HBCU Basketball League." *Vice Sports,* 20 June 2017. sports.vice.com. Accessed 31 July 2018.

CHAPTER 8. UPHILL BATTLES IN WOMEN'S BASKETBALL

1. William C. Rhoden. *$40 Million Slaves: The Rise, Fall, and Redemption of the Black Athlete*. Crown, 2006. 221–222.

2. "Lucy Harris." *Sports Reference*, n.d. sports-reference.com. Accessed 31 July 2018.

3. Rhoden, *$40 Million Slaves*, 224.

4. Mechelle Voepel. "Rebecca Lobo There from the Start." *espnW*, 15 Oct. 2014. espn.com. Accessed 31 July 2018.

5. Voepel, "Rebecca Lobo There from the Start."

6. Lena Williams. "Women's Sports; Hispanic Female Athletes Are Few and Far Between." *New York Times*, 6 Nov. 2002. nytimes.com. Accessed 31 July 2018.

7. Laura Depta. "Latin American Countries Producing the Most MLB Players." *Bleacher Report*, 1 May 2015. bleacherreport.com. Accessed 31 July 2018.

CHAPTER 9. THE LEADERSHIP GAP

1. Associated Press. "Diversity. Ethics Study Says College Sports Administration Still a White Man's Game." *USA Today*, 8 Nov. 2017. usatoday.com. Accessed 31 July 2018.

2. Donald H. Yee. "College Football Is Rigged against Black Head Coaches." *Washington Post*, 9 Dec. 2015. washingtonpost.com. Accessed 31 July 2018.

3. Gregory Clay. "Challenges Persist in Hiring Black Head Coaches in College Football." *Diverse: Issues in Higher Education*, 18 Jan. 2018. diverseeducation.com. Accessed 31 July 2018.

4. Adam Kilgore. "Oregon Rule Could Be College Football's Version of the 'Rooney Rule.'" *Washington Post*, 8 Dec. 2016. washingtonpost.com. Accessed 31 July 2018.

5. "House Bill 3118." *Oregonian*, 22 July 2009. gov.oregonlive.com. Accessed 31 July 2018.

6. Kilgore, "Oregon Rule Could Be College Football's Version of the 'Rooney Rule.'"

INDEX

ABOUT THE AUTHORS

DUCHESS HARRIS, JD, PHD

Professor Harris is the chair of the American Studies department at Macalester College and curator of the Duchess Harris Collection of ABDO books. She is the author and coauthor of recently released ABDO books including *Hidden Human Computers: The Black Women of NASA*, *Black Lives Matter*, and *Race and Policing*.

Before working with ABDO, she authored several other books on the topics of race, culture, and American history. She served as an associate editor for *Litigation News*, the American Bar Association Section of Litigation's quarterly flagship publication, and was the first editor in chief of *Law Raza*, an interactive online journal covering race and the law, published at William Mitchell College of Law. She has earned a PhD in American Studies from the University of Minnesota and a JD from William Mitchell College of Law.